# *everyday* **ENNEAGRAM**

*A Little Introduction to the
Nine Personality Types*

**DAYO AJANAKU**

T0364022

RP Minis®
Hachette Book Group
1290 Avenue of the Americas, New York, NY 10104
www.runningpress.com
@Running_Press

First Edition: September 2024

Published by RP Minis, an imprint of Hachette Book
Group, Inc. The RP Minis name and logo is a registered
trademark of Hachette Book Group, Inc.

Running Press books may be purchased in bulk for
business, educational, or promotional use. For more
information, please contact your local bookseller or the
Hachette Book Group Special Markets Department at
Special.Markets@hbgusa.com.

The publisher is not responsible for websites (or their
content) that are not owned by the publisher.

Design by Susan Van Horn

ISBN: 978-0-7624-8740-0

# CONTENTS

Introduction
What Is the Enneagram? ................. 5

## HE NINE ENNEAGRAM TYPES

*Overview* ........................... 10

*Finding Your Main Type* .......... 11

*The Type Wings* ................... 14

Type One ............................ 18

Type Two ............................ 22

Type Three .......................... 26

Type Four ........................... 30

Type Five ............................ 34

Type Six ............................. 38

Type Seven .......................... 42

Type Eight ........................... 46

Type Nine ........................... 50

esources for Beginners ................ 54

eferences ............................ 55

bout the Author ..................... 56

# INTRODUCTION
## What Is the Enneagram?

The Enneagram of Personality, more commonly known as the Enneagram, is an ancient personality typing system that draws on modern psychology and spiritual principles. The origins of the Enneagram have philosophical roots in ancient Greece and spiritually diverse influences. The word "enneagram" derives from the Greek words ἐννέα, meaning "nine," and γράμμα, meaning "written" or "drawn." This unique system places people's personalities into one of nine distinct personality types through different techniques. Whichever number you are categorized in serves as your main type. When illustrated, the Enneagram numbers are organized in a clock-like circle where numbers one through nine are ordered next to each other—with number one in the same position as it is on an analog clock—and geometric lines or arrows connect different numbers within the circle.

    If used mindfully—and in conjunction with the thought-provoking cards included in this set—the Enneagram has the power to influence the quality of your life. It can speak truth to areas of your life that are hidden behind fear and anxiety, and it can set you free from negative patterns that affect how you show up in the world and in your own life. It can enlighten you, revealing the secrets your personality holds for success, growth, and abundance.

# The Nine
# Enneagram Types

# OVERVIEW

Each of the nine Enneagram types offer unique gifts and face different challenges. You are born with your main type, yes, but it is molded into solid form as you move about the world and encounter situations that confirm it. Some people grow up in environments that encourage their type to flourish because their characteristics are beneficial to the society they live in. Others' may be stifled because their environment does not affirm their type's core desires and fears.

The objective of this book and card deck is to explore the ways you can use the Enneagram to foster growth and improvement within yourself. The goal is to learn and appreciate the gifts we offer, the ways in which certain traits may be hindering growth, and how to move in a way that improves all aspects of your life.

## FINDING YOUR MAIN TYPE

There are a few different ways to determine your main type. The most popular way is to take an Enneagram test from a credible source. I recommend Dr. Deborah Egerton's test, found on her website (www.deborahegerton.com). Dr. Egerton is an Enneagram and inclusion, diversity, equity, and anti-racism specialist, and her test recognizes and considers differences in culture and upbringing. The issue with this method is that we may not be self-aware or sure of our truth. We often choose the answers we wish were true and not the answers that actually are true. This method will work for those who are open to seeing the truth of who they are; those who are unafraid of what they may see when looking on the other side.

Another way to determine your type is by reading books like this one! Rather than asking questions, books state the descriptions of each type, and you get to determine what resonates with you. Typically, what should ring true are the type's core motivations, desires, and fears.

The last recommended approach is to participate in typing interviews with an Enneagram coach. Depending on the experience and cultural competency of the coach, this can be a helpful method. Inaccuracies can arise if the coach lacks understanding of the interviewee's societal position since they may not take such influences into account.

My advice is to explore all three of these avenues within a group of trusted Enneagram communities and refer to the corresponding cards for affirmations and thought-provoking questions to further your journey.

The Enneagram is used not to become a stereotypical version of your main type. It is used to get back to the essence of who you are and to learn how to use this knowledge when needed. It is a tool that you use depending on whatever situation, environment, and headspace you find yourself in. But do remember: You are your essence, not your type.

With all this information now in your back pocket, let's get to know the types!

## THE TYPE WINGS

An aspect of the Enneagram that further creates unique type expression is the type wings. While everyone has one main type, the expression of that type can be significantly influenced by which wings they lean on. Wings are the numbers directly next to your main type number on the Enneagram symbol. Each of the nine main types have two options for wings: Type One has Nine and Two; Type Two has One and Three; Type Three has Two and Four; Type Four has Three and Five; Type Five has Four and Six; Type Six has Five and Seven; Type Seven has Six and Eight; Type Eight has Seven and Nine; Type Nine has Eight and One. When written, wings are represented with a lowercase "w." You may see someone write "1w2" or "2w3." These translate to "Enneagram Type One with a wing number Two" and "Enneagram Type Two with a wing number Three," respectively.

Wings are the facets of your personality you use when in different social settings. You may lean on one wing when you're with your family but use the other wing when you're out with friends, at work, on a date, or in any other environment. There are forms of interactions that are acceptable with certain people that might not be acceptable with others, and your wings will assist you with creating favorable outcomes in all situations. Utilizing the influence of your wings is a fundamental tool in your Enneagram toolbelt. Much like we recommend finding your main type, it is a good idea to read up on the type wings and to discuss them with friends and family to determine which wing you favor.

Wings aren't always in use, though. You have the option of engaging one wing over the other, or you can use both simultaneously—or even use neither. Wings help you answer the question of *Who do I need to be in order to thrive in this environment?*

# TYPE

## 1

Given the nicknames the Perfectionist or the Reformer, the first type of the Enneagram is full of integrity and the need to always improve. People with the Type One personality are known as reliable and detail oriented, and for having incredibly high standards. Ones see everything as black and white—this can lead to internal battles, deciding what lies within their boundaries. Above all, Ones value honesty and truth.

Type Ones may experience bouts of hypercriticism because they see the flaws of the world clearly. Like the nickname suggests, many may also struggle with perfectionism.

**1w9—The Optimist**: *Focused with obtaining harmony through peaceful means.*

**1w2—The Activist**: *Endeavors to always advocate for, help, and support others.*

# TYPE **1**'S CORE:

### *Desire*
Being seen as a good person by
themselves and others.

### *Fear*
Being seen as bad or corrupt.

### *Motivation*
Returning order to the world.

## *Struggles*

Self-righteousness.
Hypercriticism of themselves
and others. Perfectionism.

---

*Individuals who share the
Type One personality structure
include Michelle Obama, Gandhi,
Nelson Mandela, and Brené Brown.*

The Type Two is sometimes called the Helper or the Giver. Twos are highly relational people who are gentle, soft, and kind. They are cheerleaders, supporting loved ones in whatever they do. If they are not careful, they can easily neglect themselves in their pursuit of helpfulness. Acceptance is vital to the Type Two. It is important that those around them feel unconditionally loved, and they can shape-shift and adapt to provide this—sometimes to their detriment.

Twos are the best people to go to for advice because they are active listeners. They are gifted with the ability of assessing and meeting people's needs. Although, this can feel smothering for those on the receiving end, especially if the help is unsolicited.

---

TYPE TWO WINGS

**2w1—The Companion:** *Encouraging and supportive of everyone including themselves.*

**2w3—The Host:** *Adaptable, flexible, and responsive; an optimist.*

# TYPE **2**'S CORE:

### *Desire*
Being seen as a loving person by themselves and by others.

### *Fear*
Being unloved.

### *Motivation*
To be useful and irreplaceable in the eyes of others.

### *Struggles*

Setting boundaries.
Meeting their own needs and
being preoccupied with
the needs of others.

Individuals who share the Type
Two personality structure include
Desmond Tutu, Nancy Reagan, Maya
Angelou, and Jimmy Carter.

The Enneagram Type Three is sometimes called the Achiever or the Performer. They are driven to reach success but only in the way that fits their environment's definition of it. Not all Threes are motivated by material things—especially if they are not status symbols in their community. Threes long for affirmation and admiration for their achievements.

Threes are charismatic people who lead with enthusiasm and energy. They make incredible entrepreneurs because of their adaptability and drive. Once they reach retirement, Threes may find it hard to rest and enjoy the life they have built because of how attached their identity is to their career. Threes may also struggle with competitiveness. They can create unwanted competition due to their desire to be the best.

---

## TYPE THREE WINGS

**3w2—The Enchanter:** *Warm, caring, and efficient at making dreams a reality.*

**3w4—The Expert:** *Emotionally mature and aware; always striving to improve.*

# TYPE **③**'S CORE:

### *Desire*
To be seen as a valuable person
by themselves and by others.

### *Fear*
Being seen as worthless.

### *Motivation*
Creating a life that is worthwhile.

### *Struggles*
Placing their worth and
value in what they do and not who

they are, leading to burnout and overworking. Not knowing their limits and striving for positive feedback no matter the cost. Answering the question, *Who am I outside of my work?* Competitiveness.

Individuals who share the Type Three personality structure include Michael Jordan, Oprah Winfrey, Justin Bieber, and Reese Witherspoon.

# TYPE

## 4

The Type Four is sometimes called the Individualist or the Creative. Authenticity is of utmost importance to Type Fours. They actively avoid fads and trends, and they would rather miss out on experiences simply because too many others are involved. They do not want to be a carbon copy of anyone, and they treasure their individuality. Many artists and actors are Fours. They care deeply about their chosen craft and want to inspire others to also do good, creative work. Fours are gifted at expressing the human experience in innovative ways. A life that feels disingenuous is a life the Type Four cannot peacefully live in.

Another defining characteristic of a Type Four is their ability to tap into complex, even taboo, emotions and feelings. The high side of this is that they can be incredibly empathetic, compassionate, and understanding. The low side is the Four's tendency to get stuck in a dark, melancholic headspace.

TYPE FOUR WINGS
4w3—The Enthusiast: *Driven to understand everyone and to obtain authenticity.*
4w5—The Free Spirit: *Curious and connected; carries the ability to remain authentic no matter what.*

# TYPE ❹'S CORE:

### *Desire*
To be seen as a special person to themselves and by others.

### *Fear*
That they are incomplete.

### *Motivation*
The pursuit of difference, expressed primarily through creative means.

### *Struggles*

Isolating themselves and
becoming moody when life
becomes difficult.
Becoming overly emotional
and hyperfocused on
their inner world.

---

Individuals who share the Type Four
personality structure include Rumi,
Rihanna, Billie Eilish, and Kanye.

The Type Five is sometimes called the Investigator or the Observer. Fives are known as the experts of the Enneagram. They desire to accumulate all the information possible to feel equipped enough to manage the world around them. They find great joy in researching topics that interest them for the sake of knowledge. Type Fives are also known to live a minimalist lifestyle since they can survive on very little. They are excellent at saving money and being thrifty, but

his can be seen as stinginess
by others.

The Type Five has the innate ability
to be objective. On the low side, this
objectivity can look like compartmen-
talization of feelings and emotions. On
the high side, it can look like the ability
to remain neutral in order to provide
unbiased feedback and perspective.

---

**TYPE FIVE WINGS**

5w4—The Philosopher: *Attentive and
focused; a creative problem solver.*

5w6—The Troubleshooter:
*Even-tempered; passionate about
connecting the dots and finding solutions.*

# TYPE **5**'S CORE:

### *Desire*
To be seen as a
competent person.

### *Fear*
Being seen as incapable or
lacking the necessary knowledge
to understand the world
around them.

### *Motivations*
Knowledge and mastery.

## *Struggles*

Retreating into their mind to avoid having to expending their personal resouces. Creating rigid boundaries, which can result in missing out on experiences. Acknowledging and meeting their own needs.

---

Individuals who share the Type Five personality structure include Albert Einstein, Jane Goodall, Shonda Rhimes, and Neil deGrasse Tyson.

# TYPE

**6**

The Enneagram Type Six is sometimes called the Loyalist or the Loyal Skeptic. They are dependable, hard-working, trustworthy, and responsible. Like the Type One (the Reformer), Type Six is excellent at spotting problems. However, what fuels this acute troubleshooting ability is their anxiety about things that could possibly go wrong. Another defining characteristic of a Type Six is their inner committee. This inner committee offers different viewpoints and ideas, and Type Sixes access this committee in decision-making.

Unlike any other, Type Six has two distinct types within itself: the Phobic Six and the Counterphobic Six. Phobic Sixes manage their anxiety by moving away from and avoiding their triggers, while Counterphobic Sixes manage their anxiety by springing into action against the fear.

---

**6w5—The Guardian:** *Fights for truth and to correct unethical processes, systems, etc.*

**6w7—The Confidant:** *Loyal, engaged, and intensely concerned with the wellbeing of others.*

# TYPE **6**'S CORE:

### *Desire*
To be seen as a committed person

### *Fear*
Being left without security or support in their time of need.

### *Motivation*
Ensuring they have guidance and direction in their lives.

### *Struggles*
Persistent anxiety.
Lack of self-trust.

---

Individuals who share the Type Six personality structure include Dre Johnson (*Black-ish*), Sarah Jessica Parker, Khadijah James (*Living Single*), and Tom Hanks.

# TYPE

**7**

The Enneagram Type Seven is sometimes called the Enthusiast or the Adventurer. They embrace spontaneity and often have diverse interests and hobbies. Sevens are motivated by the desire to maintain freedom. They are typically extroverts, but this may vary depending on several factors. Sevens have a tendency to start projects, ventures, etc., they never finish. They will often exert themselves due to their fear of missing out on new, exciting opportunities and experiences.

Like Type Threes (the Achiever), Sevens are the "yes" type. However, the desire to keep life interesting is often a mechanism to avoid painful experiences. Unlike Type Fours (the Individualist), Sevens do not enjoy dark, heavy emotions. They want to avoid going too deep out of fear of getting stuck. However, Type Fours and Type Sevens both possess inherent creativity and an active imagination.

---

## TYPE SEVEN WINGS

**7w6—The Pathfinder:** *Productive and collaborative; positive even when in difficult situations.*

**7w8—The Opportunist:** *Charismatic and self-assured; level-headed in all circumstances.*

# TYPE **7**'S CORE:

### *Desire*
To be a person with freedom
and options.

### *Fear*
Not being able to experience all
that life has to offer.

### *Motivation*
Ensuring that they are living an
exciting life.

### *Struggles*

Becoming distracted by the number of interests and projects they have on their plate. Slowing down long enough to feel their emotions. Completing mundane tasks.

---

Individuals who share the Type Seven personality structure include Tiffany Haddish, Kevin Hart, Russell Brand, and Miley Cyrus.

# TYPE

## 8

The eighth Enneagram type is sometimes called the Challenger or the Protector. Type Eights meet conflict and threats head on and with strength and power. They often come off as unafraid and unintimidated. Eights can make great leaders due to their charm and persuasive nature. Eights are champions of justice and endeavor to right wrongdoings. You will often see this type at the forefront of a proverbial battle, fighting for others. As noble as this sounds, this can be perceived as controlling for those they are fighting for.

Deep down, Eights yearn to feel safe and protected themselves. On the inside, they are not so tough. In health, they are described as tender and soft but not in a way that makes them vulnerable to attack. They easily melt into the arms of those they love and trust when the world seems too heavy to bear. Eights desire to be held in both their strength and in their vulnerabilities.

8w7—The Nonconformist: *Inspiring and innovative; an optimistic leader.*

8w9—The Diplomat: *Perceptive, supportive, and protective of all.*

# TYPE **8**'S CORE:

### *Desire*
To be seen as a strong person to themselves and by others.

### *Fear*
That if they are not strong, they will be harmed by those around them.

### *Motivation*
Ensuring harm does not meet them, weakness does not stop them, and that they are in full

control of their environment and situations.

### *Struggles*

Avoiding vulnerabilities at all costs. Saying no when they believe that no one else is capable or strong enough to do the job.

---

Individuals who share the Type Eight personality structure include Serena Williams, Alexandria Ocasio-Cortez, Bernie Mac, and Winston Churchill.

The last type in the Enneagram, Type Nine, is sometimes called the Peacemaker or the Mediator. Nines bring balance to the Enneagram. They are typically slow moving and mellow, possessing grace and serenity. They tend to be liked by everyone they meet. Their Zen-like energy is a tool they utilize when serving as mediator. They are easygoing and tolerant of all people, no matter the differences.

Similar to Type Twos (the Helper), Nines are heavily focused on relationships. To ground themselves, they often cling to their people in moments of high stress or conflict. Like Type Fours (the Individualist), Nines have a rich inner world. They are deep thinkers and seekers of meaning who are keenly connected to the world around them.

**9w8—The Advisor:** *Determined to find truth and justice; steadfast.*

**9w1—The Negotiator:** *Focused on helping others; holds a harmonious and balanced perspective.*

# TYPE **9**'S CORE:

### *Desire*
To be seen as a whole and
balanced person to themselves
and by others.

### *Fear*
Experiencing loss and separation
from a lack of peace or harmony.

### *Motivation*
Ensuring that they are creating a
harmonic life free of conflict.

### *Struggles*
Making decisions—especially
ones that may result in
disharmony. Being unaware
of their own wants and needs
because they have suppressed
them in order to avoid problems.

---

Individuals who share the Type Nine
personality structure include Barack
Obama, Janet Jackson, Ariana Grande,
and Mister Rogers.

# *Resources for Beginners*

## ANTI-RACISM AND ENNEAGRAM COACHES / COMPANIES

Danielle Fanfair / Confusion to Clarity

Deborah Egerton / Trinity Transition Consultants

Jessica D. Dickson / The Antiracist Enneagram

Milton Stewart / Kaizen Careers, Coaching and Consulting

The Narrative Enneagram

## BOOKS

*Know Justice Know Peace*
by Dr. Deborah Egerton

*The Complete Enneagram*
by Beatrice Chestnut

*The Enneagram for Black Liberation*
by Chichi Agorom

*The Wisdom of the Enneagram*
by Don Richard Riso and Russ Hudson

## INSTAGRAM PAGES TO FOLLOW

@danielle_fanfair
@doitforthegrampodcast
@enneagrameverything
@enneahealth
@jessicaddickson
@jessicaddicksoncoaching
@ninetypesco
@typesinblackink
@yourenneagramcoach

## YOUTUBE CHANNELS

Abbey Howe
Frank James
You've Got a Type

## *References*

https://abbeyhowe.com/
https://blog.prepscholar.com/
https://cloverleaf.me/
https://enneagramexplained.com/
https://enneagramgift.com/
https://personalitygrowth.com/

https://personalityhunt.com/
https://theenneagramacademy.com/
https://thepleasantpersonality.com/
https://www.crystalknows.com/
https://www.enneagraminstitute.com/
https://www.indeed.com/
https://www.integrative9.com/
https://www.narrativeenneagram.org/
https://www.truity.com/
https://www.yourenneagramcoach.com/

## About the Author

**DAYO AJANAKU** is the creator and owner of The Black Enneagram and is an Enneagram Type One. She works to create and share Enneagram content that is accessible for communities of color. Dayo's hope is that you will be able to find your type, learn more about how you relate to it, and see the diverse ways the types show up in the world.